Easter Sunrise

*I dedicate this book to Cliff and Jean Hampton
who live in the light of Easter and validate it
with their thoughts, words and deeds.*

J. John

Easter
Sonrise

TRIANGLE

First published in Great Britain in 1998 by
Triangle, SPCK, Marylebone Road, London NW1 4DU

Bible quotations are from the New International Version © 1973,
1978 and 1984.

All pictures supplied by Photodisc except for p8, *Christ of St John
of the Cross*, courtesy of The Burrell Collection, Glasgow.

British Library Cataloguing-in-Publication Data
A catalogue record for this book is available from the British
Library

ISBN 0-281-05135-6

Typeset by Nigel Baines
Printed in Hong Kong by Dah Hua

The
end as
beginning

Have you ever wondered why Christians choose the symbol of the cross for their faith? What other belief in the world, whose major theme is love, has as its emblem a gallows, gas-chamber or electric chair? The cross is a symbol of the cruellest and possibly the most painful form of execution ever invented by humankind. It originated in 600 BC and was abolished by the Emperor Constantine in the fifth century.

No other death has raised a fraction of the interest or concern as that of Jesus Christ. Think of a biography – usually the death comes in the last chapter, often on the last page and even in the last paragraph. It's interesting that of all the things Jesus could have asked us to remember, He instructed us to remember His death.

Many writers have tried to face the question 'Who is Jesus Christ?' and communicate His significance for each generation. Despite our critical generation, which has shattered the reputations of many great personalities of the past, Jesus Christ remains a dominant figure. There is no denying the importance of Jesus in the history of the world and in the lives of over 1,000 million people in the world today, who call Him by such titles as King, Lord, Saviour, Son of God.

History is full of people who have claimed to come from God, or to be gods, or to bring messages from God. But how do we decide whether any of them are right in their claims? Two good tests are reason and history – reason because everyone has it, and history because everyone lives it.

Reason suggests that if any one of these people did actually come from God, then God would support the messenger's claim by pre-announcing their coming. Further, if God did not give His support there would be nothing to prevent any impostor from appearing in history claiming: 'I come from God!' In such cases there would be no objective historical way of testing the messenger. We would have only their word for it, and they could be wrong!

When people travel to a foreign country as diplomats, that country may request their passports and other documents as testimony that they represent another government. If such proofs of identity are required of delegates from other countries, reason certainly ought to demand a similar level of scrutiny of messengers who claim to come from God. To each claimant reason asks: 'What record was there before you were born that you were coming?'

In the Old Testament, written many hundreds of years before the birth of Christ, one finds clearly predicted the virgin birth of the Messiah, His life, work and death. There are 322 references relating to this person to come. Can one doubt that the ancient predictions point to Jesus? No! Why? Because Jesus fulfilled every single one of them.

When Jesus appeared, He struck history with such impact that He split it in two, dividing it into two periods, one before His coming, BC (Before Christ), the other after it, AD (Anno Domini – the year of our Lord).

Another interesting observation that separates Jesus from all other leaders is that every person who ever came into the world came 'to live'. Jesus came 'to die'. Death was a stumbling block to Socrates – it interrupted his teaching. But to Jesus, death was His goal, and the new beginning. Few of His words are really understood without reference to His cross.

For 2,000 years Jesus has caused divergent opinions. But the first Christians stated emphatically, 'we preach Christ crucified'. Jesus is admired, loved and adored by millions. He is the reason why Christianity lives and thrives in the world today. Although He scarcely ever went beyond the confines of His own land, His teachings have influenced the thinking and lives of millions throughout the world. This is all the more remarkable because from a human point of view He was a public failure and died a disgraceful death.

Despite this, Jesus fascinates and remains the most important person the world has ever seen.

Did Jesus die or was He killed? Jesus said: 'No one takes my life from me, I lay it down of my own free will.'

Jesus accused

The guards arrest Jesus and take him to trial. The governor publicly states that the prisoner is an innocent man: 'I find no reason to condemn this man, therefore I will have him whipped and set free.' Was there ever a more illogical 'therefore' uttered?

Imagine a scene in a court of law today. The
defendant is in the dock, and the evidence given. The
jury retires to consider the evidence and returns with
a 'not guilty' verdict. The prisoner smiles, sighs with
relief and waves to family and friends in the court.

The judge stands and tells the court: 'This man has
been tried and the jury declares him innocent. I have
therefore decided to sentence him to three months'
imprisonment.'

Unbelievable! Declared innocent, Jesus is taken to the
barrack yard where He is scourged – whipped with

leather thongs to which there were sharp pieces of metal attached. The scourging ripped His flesh and caused intolerable pain. Jesus then has to proceed, compelled to carry the crossbar to the execution site, Golgotha. On arrival, Jesus is stripped naked and laid on the ground. The cross beam is placed under His shoulders. His arms are outspread, tied and nailed to the cross. The crossbar with Jesus is lifted and secured to an upright post. His feet are tied and nailed to the upright post. He hangs there for three hours.

A most remarkable painting is Salvador Dali's 'Christ of St John of the Cross', which hangs in the Glasgow Art Gallery. The cross itself is massive and looms over the world. The figure on the cross is strong and Christ seems to be holding back the forces of darkness and evil, and in the foreground the earth, sea and sky are lit with a powerful new light streaming from the crucified figure.

The cross dominates the world, and the world that the artist sees is the world on which Christ looks from His cross, and seeing the world from the angle of the cross brings a new perspective.

Looking directly at the cross is difficult, because the cross is a horrifying and graphic picture of violence, brutality and pain. We may be outraged by the details of a real crime and yet be enthralled and captivated by the same details in a fictitious one. But the cross is real. It is not a fake story. The cross of Jesus is a true story of pain, agony and heartbreak – emotions we try to avoid.

By taking a look at life the way Salvador Dali tried to – looking from the cross at the world – problems do not vanish, rather their contours change. People

remain people, but seen from the cross they show up in a different light. Jesus has a unique angle on all of us.

What did His death on the cross achieve?

There are four truths about Jesus' death. First, God speaks; second, God acts; third, God enters into personal relationships with people; and fourth, God enables us to live differently.

God speaks

The cross speaks a certain word about humankind and about God. To men and women the word is 'sinful'. Sin means failing to do what God commanded us to do. Sin is not just concerned with our behaviour towards others, but also with our attitude towards God. In the cross we see the ultimate meaning of all our sin. It is anti-God and causes God pain.

The loving relationship that God wanted us to have with Him has been broken by sin. Having a broken relationship with God affects us and all our other relationships. It is as if we *all* have an overdraft of sin, and because we all have an overdraft, we cannot help each other – only someone in credit can help us. Jesus was the only one in credit. He died on a cross to somehow offer us a cheque, signed with His own blood so that our overdraft of sin, regret and disappointment can be cleared – forgiven and healed.

And on the cross God is speaking *love*. The Bible records: 'God demonstrates His own love for us in this: while we were still sinners, Christ died for us' (Romans 5.8).

By the cross God has spoken; through the cross we may know what He is like and experience His love for each one of us.

God acts

On the cross, God was doing as well as saying. He was in fact doing what He was saying. We can sum it up in one word: 'rescue'. God's action through the cross is a rescuing one, reaching down to the deepest point of every person's need. The biblical word used for rescue is 'redemption'. The Apostle Paul states it

as: 'justified freely by his grace through the redemption that came in Christ Jesus' (Romans 3.24). In the minds of Paul's original readers the idea of a redeemer would conjure up a picture of a great benefactor freeing prisoners or slaves by actually paying some ransom price for them. By the cross, the strength of God's love more than matches the power of His anger, but not at the expense of His justice, for in Jesus Christ God satisfied His righteous demand that sin be punished once and for all: 'For Christ died for sins once for all, the righteous for the unrighteous to bring you to God' (1 Peter 3.18).

Because of one victim, there is the hope of release and pardon for *all*. The cross marks God's decision within history to rescue us.

God enters into personal relationships with people

If there is a breakdown in a relationship between two parties, a mediator is required to bring them back together. Should the relationship between God and humankind break down, who is able to be mediator? Who is able to represent both God and humankind? Only someone who is both God and human. Jesus Christ became the perfect mediator. He was God's Son, so He could represent God and a man, so he could represent humankind.

The cross is the decisive movement of God towards the people He loves – you and me. The cross is love transformed to meet the needs of a desperate situation. The cross is the reunion of that which is separated. The Bible word for this state is 'reconciliation'. The cross enabled God and humankind to meet on new terms. Sin had caused an estrangement. God and humankind, as it were, had lost each other. But through the cross an entirely new

relationship has now become possible between God
and humankind and, consequently, between people.
Reconciliation can take place.

God enables us to live differently
Out of this new relationship transformation comes.
The result of being forgiven gives us the power to look
honestly at ourselves and what we are like and what
we have done. Such acceptance of the facts and the
situation of our life is the foundation of all healing.

Turning from sin and asking Christ's forgiveness gives
us the privilege of receiving His Holy Spirit. After His
resurrection, Jesus went to heaven because had He
remained on earth in His bodily human form He
could only have been in one place at any one time. He
promised that after He returned to heaven, God
would send the Holy Spirit into the world, and the
Holy Spirit would dwell within every Christian.

The Bible teaches that the Holy Spirit is an
interpreter, revealing Christ, illuminating His
teaching, strengthening us to live differently –
displaying the characteristics of love, joy, peace,
patience, kindness, goodness, faithfulness, gentleness
and self-control – what the Bible calls Fruit of the
Holy Spirit.

Easter Sonrise

On the cross the life of the most remarkable man on earth ended. But one chapter closed and another opened...

Easter Sonrise – the triumphant return of the crucified Christ. Here was the assurance that death does not grimly write on the last page of our earthly existence, *the end*, but inscribes instead with confidence, *to be continued*!

On several occasions Jesus spoke of His Resurrection: 'The Son of Man will go up to Jerusalem and be scourged, spat upon, crucified and on the third day He will rise again.'

Did He rise? If Christ did not rise, then the Apostles were either fools or frauds. Were they gullible and

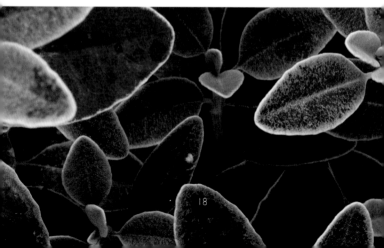

naive? In fact, they themselves were so far from being eager to believe in the Resurrection that when three women came back from the tomb with the news that it was empty and that Christ had risen, 'to their minds the story was madness' (Luke 24.11).

Such men would never be content with any second-hand evidence and they did not have to be. Later Christ came to them and they saw Him with their own eyes. They saw Him, not just then but many times thereafter. They saw Him, not at a distance but close-up. They saw Him, not in a flash, like a magician's trick, but over a space of six weeks, the period before He returned to heaven. They saw Him when there was not just one witness, or two or three, when you might suspect hallucinations, but with a dozen others, then a hundred, once two hundred and once five hundred.

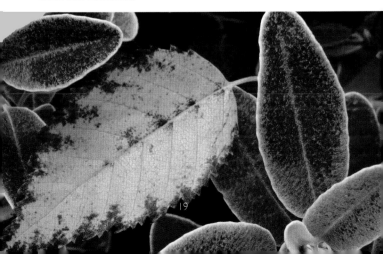

Most of the Apostles eventually died the violent death of martyrdom. Frauds do not die for their causes. We more easily believe that a person is telling the truth when they are willing to have their throat cut as witness to their testimony. The Apostles did just that!

The Resurrection is a proof, a pledge and a plea. It is a proof that Jesus Christ is the Son of God, for by defeating death, God is shown as the Ringmaster of Nature; only Jesus' cross is the key that could open the lock of death; only the Son of God could sleep in death and then through God's power stir and rise to life!

The Resurrection is a pledge that authenticates Jesus' teaching. Therefore I know all His words are trustworthy.

And finally the Resurrection is a plea for us to meet the Risen Christ with the wounds of past mistakes, errors, hurts and sins to shine with Easter forgiveness and healing.

If Jesus had not risen He would have been buried under the words, 'suffered under Pontius Pilate, died and was buried'. Christianity would have been a two-inch footnote in any encyclopaedia. But, instead, Christianity proceeded to topple great empires, to form the very framework of our civilization, to give culture the best of art and music and to become the teacher of people's conscience – it was only because the founder of Christianity rose from the grave.

If the story of Jesus' birth startles, if His teachings challenge, if His miracles amaze, if His sufferings shock, if His death crushes, His Resurrection astounds and reassures us that in Jesus there is forgiveness from the past, new life today and a hope for the future.

Conclusion

There is something in the human heart that turns almost naturally towards anniversaries. Each year in Stratford-on-Avon, in a chapel under whose slab lies the great Shakespeare, a ceremony is held. On a ledge along the wall perches a marble bust of Shakespeare busily writing. Each year on 23 April, the anniversary of his death, the old feathered quill from those stony fingers is slid out, and in slips a new quill as a symbol that Shakespeare lives on, making an impact in the literature of the world.

Good Friday is the anniversary of the death of the Son of God. But because of Easter Day we are able to stand not before the tomb of the unknown soldier, but before the known Saviour.

Knowing Jesus Christ is a life-changing experience because to know Jesus Christ is to find the meaning of life itself.

Glossary

Ash Wednesday

Ash Wednesday is the first day of Lent. At an Ash Wednesday church service, ash is marked on a participant's face in the form of a cross as a sign of penance ('penance' means expressing regret for one's wrongdoings). This is a reminder of sackcloth and ashes as a sign of penance in the Old Testament of the Bible. When a person is signed with the ash, the following words are spoken: 'Remember, dust you are and to dust you will return' (Genesis 2.14). This reminder of the mortality of the human race starts the preparation for reflection and meditation, penance and prayer for the Easter festival.

Easter

The day commemorating the Resurrection from the dead of Jesus Christ. The word 'Easter' comes from the Anglo-Saxon Spring goddess, Eostre. In the eighth century Saint Bede converted the festival of Easter into the festival of Christ's Resurrection, and the meaning of many other pagan symbols were changed to symbolize the relevance of Easter.

Eggs

For thousands of years, the Greeks, Persians and Chinese gave eggs as gifts in the spring, celebrating new life in nature.

For Christians today eggs are a symbol of new life. Eggs look dead but they contain life. In some countries eggs are painted red to symbolize Christ's blood. The chick is small, yellow and fluffy but soon grows into a large hen which will lay the eggs from which other chicks will be born. The cycle of life goes on, giving rise to the question: 'Which came first, the chicken or the egg?'

Good Friday
Good Friday is the anniversary of the crucifixion of Jesus Christ. In many churches, services are held between noon and 3pm, to reflect upon and remember the period of time Jesus hung on the cross.

The hare and the rabbit
The hare was a symbol of fertility in ancient Egypt. Today the symbol of fertility is the rabbit.

Hot cross buns
These are spiced currant buns marked with a cross, eaten on Good Friday as a symbol of remembrance of Jesus' death on the cross.

Lent
Lent is derived from the Anglo-Saxon word 'Lenten', which means Spring. Lent represents the 40-day period

of Jesus' temptation in the desert. Lent runs from Ash Wednesday to Holy Saturday. Many people, rather than fasting from food completely, fast from a pleasure such as eating chocolate, desserts or watching TV.

Maundy Thursday

The day on which Jesus' Last Supper with His disciples is remembered. He washed their feet and started the Eucharist – eating bread and drinking wine in remembrance of His death. 'Eucharist' means thankfulness.

The word 'Maundy' comes from the Latin *mandatum*, which means command. In Britain, Edward III annually washed and kissed the feet of the poor on Maundy Thursday. The Pope still washes the feet of twelve priests every year on Maundy Thursday. Queen Elizabeth II distributes special coins, Maundy money, the quantity representing every year of her age, to a number of individuals. The giving of Maundy money goes back to the fourteenth century.

Palm Sunday

Palm Sunday recalls the entry of Jesus into Jerusalem when He was welcomed by the crowds who took branches of palm trees and went out to meet Him